YOUNG ADULT

YOUNG ADULT

KYRA GUNDRED

NEW DEGREE PRESS

COPYRIGHT © 2022 KYRA GUNDRED

All rights reserved.

YOUNG ADULT

ISBN   979-8-88504-114-0 *Paperback*
           979-8-88504-742-5 *Kindle Ebook*
           979-8-88504-221-5 *Ebook*

CONTENTS

note from the author	7
husk	11
friends	13
dead things	14
the sea has other plans	16
messy love	17
loving yourself first	18
part-time	19
labor day	20
dream job	21
stress	22
dormant	24
one hundred percent	26
the process	27
notre dame	28
louie	29
the arclight	31
convenience	33
puzzle	35
sand	37
coming home	38
short term memory	40
little thoughts	41
swimming pool	42
retail therapy	43
medication	44

boxes	47
depression as a disability	48
raincoat	49
grounding exercise	50
defensive woman	52
half-asian	53
body fat	54
back to school	55
pieces	56
acknowledgements	59

NOTE FROM THE AUTHOR

When I was a kid, I felt like I was never old enough to do anything. My dad would tell me, "You have to be twenty-one to go into that bar." "You have to be sixteen to drive the car." "I can't take you with me because this is a grown-up event." I was always "too young," "not old enough," "not there yet."

I was a kid floating around in a world that was meant for adults. I guess this makes sense as adults have made the world what it is. Adults have the power to make choices and changes. Adults have a say.

Occasionally I caught small glimpses of the adult world when my parents let me sit with their friends while they played poker. Or when I watched my mom get another tattoo.

In a way, I always felt five steps behind everyone else. "It's much easier to be a kid," the adults would say. "Enjoy being young, don't rush things."

But adults seemed to be living the life I wanted to experience. There was a freedom in being able to make your own choices, even if they were stupid, and to be able to go anywhere, even if you should've stayed home. There was something more whole in being an adult, something about living the human experience in its entirety.

As I grew up, I inched closer to the freedom I yearned for as a kid. I got my driver's license. I got a job and started making my own money. I moved out and went to college and started smoking. It felt weird though, more like role-play than growing up, like a puppy wearing a collar that's too big.

I went to a party once during senior year of high school. We were in some girl's garage for her birthday. All of us were only eighteen or nineteen. Her boyfriend was a tattoo artist with multiple warrants out for his arrest. Thus, his business card only said "TATTOO ARTIST: Jake." No last name. Everyone was smoking and drinking from her mom's liquor cabinet. I watched as Jake tattooed a cross on his own chest. It looked just as ridiculous as it sounds. Everyone in the garage that night felt like they were hot stuff, but I knew we weren't grown up. We were just kids with bongs and bottles.

I'm in my twenties now, and in some ways, I feel like my world has opened up the way I wanted it to when I was little. I can go to the "grown-up events." I have my own apartment and my own tattoos. I don't even go to school anymore!

However, the transition from teen to adult was more difficult than I thought it would be. I mean, they told me it wouldn't be easy, but nobody said it would be this hard. The process of entering adulthood was always presented as a checklist, something linear and ostensibly manageable: go to college, get a job, find a place to live. My reality ended up looking more like an elaborate juggling act as I tried to learn how to take care of myself, how to maintain meaningful relationships, and generally how to tune myself in to a world I was just waking up to. The personal growth that occurs when you attempt to piece together these abstract things is casually mentioned, but hardly explored. "You'll see for yourself," they say. "This is when you figure out who you are." I learned that coming of age hardly resembles that pithy John-Hughes-movie optimism.

I took to social media to do the dangerous thing: to compare my progress with that of my peers. After copious hours on Twitter, I discovered that everyone else was having a tough time with adulthood, too. Humor seemed to be the medicine of choice for our growing pains. It was easier to make people laugh with a backhanded meme than to start a heartfelt discussion about gushy feelings. Nobody seemed to talk enough about how difficult it is to grow out of your teens and begin the journey of finding out what it means to be an adult. Although anyone who knows me knows that I'm a sucker for internet comedy, I began writing poems to help me process my thoughts and experiences in a more honest, reflective way.

At first, I only wrote for me. Now, I would like to share my thoughts with people like those avid tweeters who are maybe too shy to directly admit that they feel those strong emotions, or maybe just can't seem to find the right words to describe them. I want to open up the discussion about the transition into adulthood and let other young adults know that they are not alone in their struggle. I hope that by talking about my mental health and my moments of self-discovery, other young adults will feel more comfortable sharing theirs. It is hard enough to simply get through life without the added stress of feeling alone in the experience. Literature has provided that relief for me ever since I could read, so I think it would be an honor to pass along that comfort, to carry that tradition in my own way.

Though my experiences are uniquely tailored to me as yours are to you, I hope you will find solace in reading another human admitting that it is quite hard, at times, to be human.

husk

my love and i sit on our couch,
hearts open,
guards down.
we huddle together,
sharing the nest we've made
in tender silence.

i am louder with my friends,
a parakeet rather than a mouse
chirping witty banter
chattering to amuse.

but i'm often exhausted afterwards,
like i've danced an elaborate ballet
and must recharge for the next performance.

when i am with my friends
i wear a mask,
one that feigns agreeability,
lest friendliness be lost.
where is this mask
when i am with my lover?
why is there no need
to show him i am enough?

maybe the maskless me
is the quiet mouse he sits with.
perhaps i am really a husk,
empty and wordless,
ashamed that i can't be more for him.

which is the real me—
the mouse or the parakeet?
or do i show each person in my life
a different version of myself?
do they each get a part of me
that no one else has?

friends

have a picnic at the beach with me
we can trade our favorite books
and share all our best memes
peel my skin back like a tangerine
enjoy sweet yet sour vulnerability
i'll tell you the secrets even i don't know
until i say them out loud

but when the night is over
and we're back in our own beds
will our day mean as much to you
as it did to me?
how futile it is to seek happiness
in the company of others—
my attempts at connection often feel
like striking a match
just to watch it burn away

perhaps it is more realistic to believe
that moments of joy don't have to last forever
to retain a place in my heart.
people can enrich my life without staying
and i cannot take prisoners
in the name of friendship.

if i do not see you tomorrow,
i can still find comfort in knowing
that our picnic was lovely
while it lasted.

dead things

i want to stop ruminating over dead things:
friendships,
romances,
conflicts,
promises.

i started a garden on my balcony,
a small haven of growth and potential.
colorful pots arranged on wooden tables,
enjoying open air among tree tops.
they sit, hearty and steadfast,
growing slowly and patiently
overlooking the other balconies.

i pat fresh soil around the fiddle leaf fig,
give it a place to root, to claim its own earth.
i snap a browning leaf off of the monstera,
and for a moment i feel grounded.

i turn my focus to living things
friendships
romance
promises
so i can nurture what is present
and prune away the past.

the sea has other plans

i see you there,
across the ocean

drifting in your boat
leaving the same port as i

we remain divided among currents
minimized to light signals through the fog

i remember a time when i thought
we'd be carried by the same wave

that we'd tread these waters
together

how foolish of me to forget
that the sea has other plans

messy love

my love is messy,
and can be ugly.

sometimes it doesn't fit quite right,
is too big or too small,
like a tattered sweater knit
by a well-intentioned novice.

it will be cast aside,
called names on the playground,
reduced to picking wood chips
from its tender knees.

but i know that in spite of these flaws,
my love will persist.

loving yourself first

loving yourself first
means loving them second
even when it hurts
even when you really really love them
because sometimes it is necessary to disappoint
no matter how badly we'd like to please

loving yourself first
means declining party invitations
in favor of restful nights in
showing more skin
despite sideways glances
raising your voice
in defense of your dignity
removing rose-colored glasses
to better spot red flags

loving yourself first
is more than sage advice
it is a means of survival

part-time

got a part-time job,
now i'm a full-time cog
in a capitalist machine
chasing dreams of green

i'll make your money
but you can pay me cheap
no personal life necessary,
this "family" is enough for me

i live life on the clock
yet there's never enough time
i sleep for an hour
wake up to make a dime

always working hard
'cause nothing comes free
is this paycheck meant to be
the american dream?

labor day

i've never had a labor day free.
friends ask, "what's on for the long weekend?"
i reply, "you'll find me unlocking fitting rooms
and refolding t-shirts."
only i can taste the irony,
like blood on my tongue.

that is, except for today.
today, i had labor day off work.
i slept until noon,
sat around until two,
then took a nap until six.

it felt so good
and so wrong
to do absolutely nothing.

capitalism has me brainwashed:
even on my days off
there's this underlying feeling,
an external pressure,
to be "productive,"
that i must utilize my time
to turn profit into more profit
for some already-rich suit
who will never know my name.

no, not today.
today i labor for myself.

dream job

when we were kids
and someone asked us
"what do you want to be
when you grow up?"
the answers were so impractical

"an astronaut!"
      "an artist!"

what a perfect illusion
that question created:
a world in which dreams
were one earnest wish away

but that eagerness died away
as we grew up and realized
the importance of financial stability.
would being an astronaut be worth
the accruement of student debt?
would being an artist sustain me,
and if so, for how long?

how sad is it
to be inspired not by passion
but rather by survival?

still, i hold hope
that somehow
i'll find balance

stress

one semester,
i took five classes
because that's what the counselor recommended.
it took many missed saturday nights
to catch up with the syllabus,
and a few zeroes in the grade book
to give myself time to rest.
i bought a keyboard cover for my laptop
to protect it from my tears.
"when i graduate," i said,
"i won't be stressed anymore."

soon after i graduated,
i found my first apartment
because it was time to have my own space.
it took many photo-copied pay stubs
to prove i could afford it,
and an enormous credit card bill
to make the place a home.
i often sat alone in my car, silent.
"when i move in," i said,
"i won't be stressed anymore."

but i find that i'm always stressed
by one thing or another:
bills or stains or missed events

there is never time to soak up
special accomplishments or occasions.
there is always something else
to be stressed about.

perhaps stress is not an obstacle to overcome,
but a mindset i must overwrite.

dormant

i am becoming more comfortable with dormancy.
i sit on my phone,
pretend i am looking through a window,
watching other people do the things
i'd like to be doing.
they're starting creative projects—
experimental paintings
and dollar diy's
they're traveling,
expanding perspective.
everyone seems to be finding
soul purpose in their free time.

through all of my desire,
i still sit,
consuming
rather than creating.

there's a voice in my head
telling me to get off my ass,
to seize the day,
to make something of this life.
but it is much easier
to revel in the lives of others
than to live my own.

one hundred percent

i feel like i can never put in
one hundred percent
into anything i do anymore

there was a time when my plate
was not so full
i could lose myself in
my art, my schoolwork
where did that ambitious appetite go?

lately, i've been functioning at eighty percent
i feel like i am trying to pour
from an emptying pitcher
my own glass is looking more and more
half-empty these days

how do you finish a meal
with a finger in each dish?
it seems i can't stop biting off
more than i can chew

the only way to disrupt
this anxious cycle
is to cut each task
into manageable pieces

the process

i have plenty of ambitions:
to play bass in a band with my boyfriend
maybe get a taste of stardom
to live off of my art
ditch day jobs for endless creation
to cruise on a skateboard in beach towns
and empty suburban streets

but i reach for mastery on the first try
and i always fall short.
if only i could download skills
over some wireless connection,
conjure magic from my palms.

i can't sync my fingers on the strings,
my sketches don't resemble
the final image in my head,
i'm terrified i'll fall off the board,
bruise both my shins and my pride

but fear and clumsiness and lack of time
will always stand between me and my dreams
so now i'm trying to stop courting perfection
and to fall in love with the process instead

notre dame

when i went to paris
i visited notre dame
and greeted our lady with piety,
as a guest in god's house.

but god wasn't home that day.

and though i saw him
on paintings and tapestries
on post cards and keychains
i did not feel *him*—
just history
contaminated with commercialism.

i feel his presence more
in my backyard at sunrise,
in the hills i drive past
on the I-5 south,
in the living room on christmas morning.

maybe god doesn't care much for
the grandeur of a church.
maybe he prefers to be seen
in the everyday beauty
people pass on their way there.

louie

one night, while i was at work
i received a photo of a coyote
with my missing cat, louie, in its mouth.
we let him outside a week ago for his nightly outing
and he never came back.
i cried off my eyeliner in the break room,
looking more and more like an animal myself
as i wept for him.

i wanted to be angry at the coyote
for killing our cat
for robbing me of a beloved friend
but its face was so gentle.
there was no malice in its eyes.
it must have been a mother,
trying to feed its pups.
after all,
what is there for wildlife to eat
in suburbia?

i realized i could neither blame
the coyote
for following basic instinct
nor the cat
for having an adventurous spirit

at night i hear the pack
howling behind the hills

and i no longer feel angry,
but i still miss louie
every day

the arclight

my favorite movie theater stood on sunset blvd
a house of culture amidst tall corporate buildings
q&a sessions with filmmakers and
occasional celebrity spottings
made it a place of wonder
(rappers hidden in the back row of the auditorium,
actors shamelessly flirting with my mom)
where imagination and reality
blended together

my family celebrated christmas by going to see a movie
almost every year
hot dogs, popcorn, sour candy
after holiday dinner

but the pandemic began,
everything closed,
including our favorite movie theater.
the windows were boarded up
like eyes pulled shut
on a great urban treasure.

we step out to see our first movie since quarantine.
the arclight in sherman oaks has not closed
like the tragic fate of the one on sunset blvd,
but rather, has been converted to a chain.
(no pop star in the elevator this time)
they didn't even bother redecorating—
new logos, signage, and menu cards
were placed over the old ones,

imposters with poor disguises,
and the same curtains and fairy lights
hung morbidly outside each auditorium.

we conduct the usual rituals
hot dogs, popcorn, sour candy
but the experience is lackluster
in the skeleton of what once was.

convenience

i love the modern age
if i don't think about it too hard.

i can chat with someone from miles away,
and look at photos of tigers whenever i want to.

anything i can think to buy is only ever a click away
and my package will be at the door tomorrow morning.

i can pack disposable cutlery with my lunch
so i don't have to wash anything later.

then i realize thinking "too hard" about it
is thinking about it at all.

all of my personal information
is a google search away.

the person delivering my package
isn't paid a livable wage.

landfills are packed
with single use plastic like mine.

instant gratification
has become the norm.

supply will be met
by any means possible.

we have never been more connected
yet we have never been more vulnerable.

our plastic will outlive us
and probably the planet too.

modern conveniences
have bred modern disasters.

when the global dread gets the best of me,
i can't help but feel complicit.

puzzle

we slowly assemble a thousand-piece puzzle,
clumps of completion in some spots
and large empty areas in others

he tapes the puzzle's image on the wall
like a road map

we'd find familiar pieces
"this could be connected to that,
we'll figure it out eventually"
i wish we treated all of our worries with such patience
"it will make sense eventually"
sometimes two pieces just need to be pushed closer together
some pieces only make sense once you've moved to the next cluster
some pieces just need to be placed last

we talked about feeling aimless, a bit confused
figuring out what we want out of the world around us
finding how to fit ourselves into the puzzle
how does one do that
without a box top as a guide?

i don't have time for puzzles now
my patience has long worn thin
how i wish i could sit down

place each piece like a prayer,
      like a promise
and trust that the bigger picture
will become clearer in the end.

sand

i went to the beach today
watched as the tide kissed the shore,
urged the land to become sea.
but the sand cannot choose where it will end up.
some grains will never touch the ocean.
others will be swallowed by it.

sometimes i feel like
a grain of sand:
tiny, helpless,
unimportant in the grand scheme of things.

but i'm learning to be okay with being small.
i don't have to be important
to be meaningful in my own way.

coming home

i have two homes:
my apartment in the city
and the house in the suburbs i grew up in.

every few weeks or so
i'll make the sixty-mile drive to my parents' house
when there's a celebration
or when i'm simply homesick

sometimes it's strange
to have my heart in two places.
the difference feels more temporal
than geographical.
my homes make a venn diagram of time:
one side is the past,
childhood and development;
the other the future,
adulthood and potential;
with this awkward adolescence in the center,
the present,
where i am simultaneously
child and adult.

i leave the GPS on
though driving is more muscle memory
than actual navigation.
coming home
has always felt natural to me.

i fumble for the silver keys
next to the brass ones for my apartment
(mama always preferred silver over gold)
and open the door
to nostalgia,
leave the phone off of the hook;
leave the future on hold.

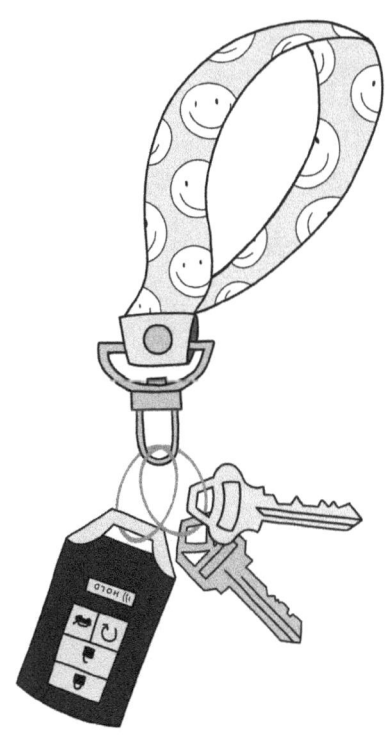

short term memory

my memories are like bubbles:
they disappear as quickly as they take shape.

i try to recall
why i walked into this room
what i was looking for
what we were just talking about
and

it escapes me.

little thoughts

little thoughts run across
my echoing cranium
pit pat pit pat
one after another
tiny socked feet on carpet.

they whisper in the background
hushed worries,
tough questions,
just loud enough for me to hear:
i'm all out of ideas,
i've lost my touch,
does anyone like me anymore?

pit pat pit pat
tiny socked feet on carpet
in my empty brain house.

swimming pool

living alone feels like
wading to the deep end of the pool
and realizing my toes
no longer touch the bottom

how will i float?
take care of a body
so dependent on others?

i tread water
and force myself
to do the laundry
to take a shower
to eat something

but some days
i am so tired
i would rather sink

retail therapy

i swing open the front door
snatch up my cardboard box

i've spent another sleepless night
shopping online

this is my reward—a video game
for passing that exam

a fresh pair of shoes
for working overtime

another house plant
for picking myself up off the floor

good job, me!
here's a treat, an incentive to keep up the good work

but will these things fill the hole in my chest?
will they give me the sense of control i crave?

maybe if i place another order
for a hoodie, a purse, a pair of patterned socks

i can add to the landfill
in my ribcage,
pretend that wholeness
can be purchased

medication

1
i peer inside the plastic bottle
see i have two pills left
        one dose
i swallow the little green-striped pills,
toss the bottle into the trash,
hear the *clang* as it lands,
pray that the pharmacy will have the refill ready tomorrow.

0
no word from the pharmacy
my first day without a dose
i try not to think about the loss
like a dog distracting itself from the absence of a bone
i put the sadness on the shelf today:
i kept my composure at work
was patient with rude strangers
even completed a grocery run—
maybe i don't need this medication after all

-1
i woke up with a dull ache in my head
behind the walls of my skull
between the folds of my brain
maybe it'll go away with a tall glass of water
and a breakfast heartier than eggo waffles
i wonder when i'll break,
when the withdrawal will set in
maybe i'm thinking about it too hard

-2
i am sobbing on my bedroom floor
if there was any streak of rationality yesterday,
it is gone now
replaced with vague, loathsome whispers
that are hardly grounded in reality
everyone hates me

    nothing i make is good

  i am not good
my brain is a half-packed bento box,
a printer with just one cartridge empty,
something important is missing

-3
i explain my dosage to the pharmacist over the phone
10 + 20 = 30 milligrams
she tells me the order can't be processed
i try my best not to start shouting
that i need this medication
that i am spiraling as we speak
that my doctor has already approved a damn refill
we reach an understanding
i send my boyfriend to pick up the prescription
i think i'd have a meltdown in the middle of walmart

30
i can feel myself rebalancing
a stone is lifted off my chest

my brain feels like a freshly stocked fridge again
the panic is subsiding
the claws are retracting
i feel whole once more
what a stupid thing to depend on,
little green-striped pills
how frustrating, how fragile
to have a brain that self-sabotages

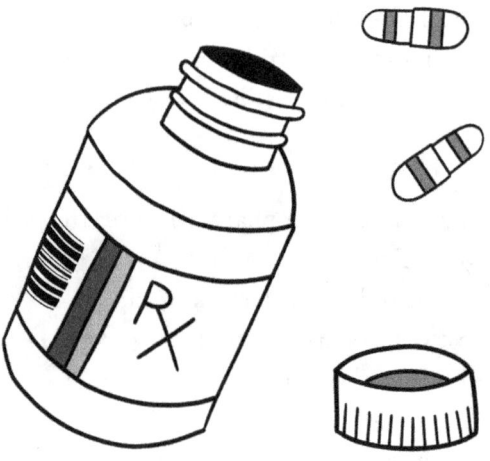

boxes

i keep myself sane by putting things in boxes
my junk, my clutter, childhood trinkets, various pills
trash overdue for throwing away
my problems, my worries

my junk, my clutter, childhood trinkets, various pills
perhaps the cause of
my problems, my worries
my thoughts won't get so tangled if i keep them in a box

perhaps the cause of
the would'ves, could'ves, should'ves
is the idea that my thoughts won't get so tangled if i keep
them in a box
maybe i should let them fly around the room?

the would'ves, could'ves, should'ves:
trash overdue for throwing away.
maybe i should let them fly around the room?
no, i keep myself sane by putting things in boxes

depression as a disability

i didn't think of depression as a disability
   until i realized that
   not everyone has to part curtains of fog
   to see the day's sunlight

   until i realized that
   my ceaseless exhaustion
   has nothing to do with sleep

   until i realized that
   it should not take more than an hour
   to make a phone call
   to get out of bed
   to convince myself to eat breakfast

on my worst days, i feel defective
like my head isn't screwed on quite right

but my body has built this house
and i am determined to live in it
for as long as i can

raincoat

no matter the forecast
i wrap my tender heart
in a yellow raincoat
before leaving the house

tears, anger, pain, grief
will roll right off my back

when customers are crass
    traffic is ruthless
    the news is grim
i remain dry, warm in my raincoat

i'm tired of absorbing
more than my heart can handle

grounding exercise

make a list of things that make life worth living:
    breakfast foods
    cats that snooze in sunbeams
    music that makes my heart sing along
    nature taking back what is rightfully hers
    knowing that i have time—that we have time—to
    explore the unknown

count the things you are grateful for:
    a roof over my head so i can hear the rain instead of
    feeling it
    a support system of people who can give me
    a tight warm hug that squeezes me back together when
    i'm falling apart
    pocket change i can spend on giant pretzels and
    fruit smoothies
    strangers who don't mind letting me say hi to their dog
    my favorite record store, which thankfully survived
    the pandemic

indulge in all of your senses
ground yourself in this physical plane:
    the sun feels warm on my skin as i drive on a
    summer day
        (wonderful with the combined scent of sunscreen)
    my body sinks into the mattress as i put myself to bed
        (the only thing that could beat this would be snuggling
        into a cloud)
    i bury my face in my cat's fur, inhaling gently
        (she smells like a teddy bear)

i watch the california hills from the passenger seat
  (bonus points if it has just rained, the brush green
  instead of brown)
the starbucks across the street finally has my favorite
drink on the menu,
  (iced peach green tea lemonade—i sip it slowly, like a
  hummingbird to nectar)
i hear my dog snoring softly from his bed as i watch
a movie
  (i marvel at the delicacy of breathing)

remember when life feels too big to handle,
there is solace to be found in life's little pleasures

defensive woman

i dress in the morning
tactfully make my body less desirable
i did not ask for large breasts
or wide hips
but i compensate for them everyday
downplay them with large t-shirts and baggy sweatpants
so nobody gets the "wrong idea"
so nobody thinks i'm inviting the attention
i receive, regardless of what i am wearing.
i remember that i was not safe in pajamas,
that even a full suit of armor would not meet my needs,
that the way i dress can only *decrease*
the probability of danger,
cannot ever assure that i get home safe.

some days i choose to flaunt the features i usually hide
i wear a sports bra as a top
and leggings that hug my ass just right
to say, "i am still proud of this body,
you do not have permission to touch me
no matter how i'm dressed."

half-asian

my mother is
chinese and filipino;
my father is
german and norwegian.
my skin is pink,
and my eyes are hooded.

people don't believe me
when i tell them i'm half-asian.
"you don't *look* asian," they sneer.
what a strange thing to say—
like i'm a watered-down stereotype.
as if being asian requires
yellow skin
and monolids

my grandmother travelled from manila to illinois
frequented the food markets in chinatown
spent long afternoons playing mahjong with her family
shared stories at the table over filipino feasts
took great pride in her chinese family name

i am asian because
i carry this heritage with me
behind my eyes
beneath my skin
and that's all the qualification i need.

body fat

i'm fatter than i was before

the pouch on my belly protrudes through my jeans
(i don't remember such difficulty in fastening that button)
and there's a pocket of fat under my chin
(my jawline used to be more pronounced)

i try to think of it as "happy" fat,
fat that indicates that i am eating well.
maybe not "well" as in "healthy,"
but "well" as in "i'm eating things that make me happy."

i eat when i celebrate
and when i'm with people i love
i love trying new foods
and feeling well fed

perhaps a bit of fat on my body is a small price to pay for that joy.

back to school

it's back-to-school season.
kids cross the streets in herds
big vibrant backpacks
on small frames.

the advertisements start
as soon as july ends.
there's a corner of the store
dedicated to pencils and folders,
and the mall dictates the coolest
cut of jean for the year

i will not be going
back to school this season.
i have served my time,
bought countless pencils,
outgrown numerous pairs of jeans,
and now,
it just feels like august.

pieces

i like to dye my hair vibrant colors.
sometimes i'll find a hair
that doesn't match the ones on my head
and i think about the person i was when i dyed it:
a purple hair in the boxes of stuff i took to college
a blonde hair on the first jeans i bought for my new body
a red hair on the leggings i wear to work.

i've spent my life taking pieces
from the personalities i liked best:
generational pop stars
and manic pixie dream girls
i am a conglomerate of stolen traits.
sometimes i find pieces of the real me—
a flower sprouting through the cracks
of the bricks i've laid down for myself
i sort through my tics,
my pet peeves, my passions
i am the culmination of everything
i've ever loved or enjoyed.
is there any part of me that is organic?
that is resistant to influences
by superficial sources?
pieces of me that are *just* me?

for years i had convinced myself
i liked the middle pieces of the brownie pan

but now i know i love the edges best.
i watched hours and hours of rom-coms on tv
before i could admit to myself that i didn't enjoy the genre.
i hope these small acts of honesty
will help me get closer to who i am.

ACKNOWLEDGMENTS

Thank you to my parents, Tom and Miriam, for your endless love and support. Thank you for always championing my dreams and empowering me to be my truest self.

Thank you to Max, my best friend and confidant, for sticking out the writing process with me. Your patience and love have carried me through this project.

Thank you to Erika Nichols-Frazer, my developmental editor, for giving me the courage to find my voice. My fears in starting my manuscript were assuaged by your gentle guidance.

Thank you to Kristin Gustafson, my marketing and revisions editor, for fortifying my vision and ultimately helping me to grow as a writer. Thank you for also showing me that writing can be (and should be!) a fun experience.

Thank you to Eric Koester of the Creator Institute for reaching out to me with this golden opportunity. This book wouldn't exist if you hadn't invited me to the Book Creators program. Thank you for putting me on the path of authorship.

Thank you to all of the kind folks at New Degree Press for all their hard work in making this story in my head a bona fide book.

Finally, a special thank you to everyone who pre-ordered a copy of my book and donated to my pre-launch campaign. Thank you very much for reminding me there are so many people in my communities who believe in me and my work.

Alyssa Gundred
Arloa & Jim Gundred
Bonnie Bernardi
Caitlyn Kelly
Christopher Pierce
Connor Williams
Craig Relyea
Don Herington
Em Flosi
Eric Koester
Francisco Hernandez
Hailey Siemantel
Iñigo Abaroa
James Carli
Jessica Contreras
John O'Brien
Juniper Iris
Kacie Rogan
Kamylle Paddio
Kari Sandhaas
Kirk Lane
Laurie Johnson
Lois Stewart
Macauley Johnson
Madeline McClain
Madison Robbins
Maria Villegas
Marisol Velazquez
Matt Gundred
Max Contreras
Mike Matejka
Miriam & Tom Gundred
Mitchell Pumar
Patricia Nihill
Patty Contreras
Savannah Hawkins
Sean Nix
Simone Christian
Skye Aldrin
Spencer Reckon
Tame Sauitufuga
Virginia Gundred
William & Erika Martinez